JUMBO JETLINERS

Boeing's 747 and the wide-bodies

JUMBO JETLINERS

Boeing's 747 and the wide-bodies

Photography NORMAN PEALING
Data MIKE SAVAGE

OSPREY
AEROSPACE

Published in 1991 by Osprey Publishing Limited
59 Grosvenor Street, London W1X 9DA

British Library Cataloguing in Publication Data

Pealing, Norman
    Jumbo jetliners.
    I. Title   II. Savage, Mike
    629.133340423

ISBN 1 85532 116 5

Editor Dennis Baldry
Page design Paul Kime
Printed in Hong Kong

Front cover A Continental Airlines
Boeing 747-100 leaves London
Gatwick Airport. In 1990 Boeing
donated the first 747 to the Seattle
Museum of Flight

Back cover A wide-bodied huddle at
London Gatwick—probably the UK's
most cosmopolitan airport due to the
number of different carriers which
operate from it

Title page A LAN-Chile Boeing
767-200ER taxying at Miami
International Airport; its 'Extended
Range' is just what is needed for the
long haul from Santiago

Right A Cathay Pacific 747, a KLM
Airbus, a Canadian Airlines
International 767 and a TWA TriStar
gather at Amsterdam Schipol
Airport—where the duty free shop
will sell you anything from a
postcard to a motor car

For a catalogue of all books published by Osprey Aerospace
please write to:

**The Marketing Department,
Octopus Illustrated Books, 1st Floor, Michelin House,
81 Fulham Road, London SW3 6RB**

The Authors

NORMAN PEALING, FRPS, FMPA began taking pictures before he entered the Royal Air Force in 1958, but his photographic portfolio was not allowed to expand into aviation subjects in the days when RAF Marham and Wittering were stuffed full of Vickers Valiant nuclear V-bombers.

In 1965 he joined the British Aircraft Corporation (BAC), and began making sales/ publicity films to promote all the company's products, which included guided weapons, satellites, military and civil aircraft. He attended many first flights and took part in the demonstration tours of the One-Eleven short-haul twinjet and the Concorde supersonic transport (SST).

In 1983 he chose to leave what had become the Weybridge Division of British Aerospace (BAe), to form his own company at Fairoaks Airport in Surrey. Norman Pealing Limited specializes in aviation photography and film/video production for advertising, sales support, public relations, publishing and television requirements.

The photographs in JUMBO JETLINERS were all taken with Hasselblad cameras and lenses, loaded with Ektachrome EPN 100 roll film.

MIKE SAVAGE is Vice President PR and Promotions for Saab Aircraft International Limited, dealing with the 340 and 2000 series of regional airliners in all markets except North America and Canada.

He began his aviation career 'sometime in the fifties', he recalls, as a student of aircraft engineering at the de Havilland Technical School in Hatfield, Hertfordshire. A commission in the Royal Air Force followed, during which he was selected for the first (and probably the last), 'all-through' jet training course at RAF Syerston in Nottinghamshire. After leaving the RAF, he fell into the employ of Handley Page Limited, where he assisted in marketing the Dart Herald airliners and promoting the Victor V-bomber.

Mike Savage has been involved in public relations and marketing ever since, having worked for the British Hovercraft Corporation (where he tried unsuccessfully to sell hovercraft to the Indian Coast Guard); the British Aircraft Corporation, where he was responsible for the initial overseas publicity of the One-Eleven short-haul airliner, and later became PR Manager for BAC's Commercial Aircraft Division during the development and proving trials for Concorde in 1972–76, and its early airline service in 1976–78; and spent six years in the Arabian Gulf, mostly with Gulf Air, until he returned to the UK and joined Saab Aircraft International in 1984.

Right Firebird: a British Airways 757 heads for the sun

Contents

747: Leader of the Jumbo Jet-set

Appropriately named *Longreach*, this Boeing 747-400 of Australian flag carrier Qantas Airways slides majestically down the glideslope into Tullamarine Airport, Melbourne. The latest of fourteen 747 versions, the first Dash 400 (powered by Pratt & Whitney PW4000 turbofans), was delivered to launch customer Northwest Airlines in January 1989; Qantas specified Rolls-Royce RB211G/H engines. The combination of drag-reducing winglets, 40,840-kg fuel capacity and the enhanced economy of the RB211G/H turbofan gives Qantas' 747-400s a maximum range of 15,410 km, enabling the carrier to operate its UK-Australia service twice daily from London Heathrow with only one stop en route—Bangkok in Thailand , or Singapore

A 747 chases its shadow as it descends on finals into Changi Airport, Singapore. Changi is a model of airport planning, its coastal location allowing unobstructed approaches over the sea and minimizing noise pollution

Left The Qantas 747-400 illustrated earlier continues its approach into Melbourne Airport. Much of the Dash 400's 2600 hours of testing confirmed the aerodynamics and structural integrity of the wingtip extensions and winglets, which reduce induced drag and thereby increase range and fuel economy. Compared with older 747 models, the Dash 400's fuel burn per seat is up to 25 per cent less; most of this improvement is due to advances in engine technology, but the contribution made by the winglets (about five per cent), is critical to the aircraft's payload/range performance

Above Leaving on a Jumbo ... in this case a Lufthansa 747-400 departing from Melbourne, destination Frankfurt. This Dash 400 is also visible in the background of the picture opposite

Two versions of Boeing's Jumbo herd on the move at Melbourne: Qantas
747-200 leads a Cathay Pacific 747-300

Left Accelerating through 185 knots, over 400 tonnes of 747-338 *City of Perth* rotates as it begins another ultra-long haul from 'down under'

Above As part of Qantas' expansion plans, their immaculate fleet of 747-200s will soon be heading off into the sunset to join other airlines in order to help finance the acquisition of up to 20 Dash 400s

Left The 747-300 introduced the extended upper deck which is also a feature of the Dash 400. Usually configured to accommodate up to 96 economy-class passengers, the EUD may alternatively be equipped with 36 first-class sleeper seats. This Dash 300 belongs to the exclusively RB211-powered 747 (and TriStar) fleet of Hong Kong's Cathay Pacific Airways. No prizes for guessing the name of the 747 operator in the foreground . . .

Above The striking livery of Fiji-based Air Pacific distinguishes this 747-200 as it taxies at Melbourne Tullamarine. Unusually, the control tower (upper left of picture), is situated away from the terminal buildings on the opposite side of the airport. A departing Qantas 767-200ER casts its shadow

Left The flight deck of the Dash 400 is configured for two-crew operation only; the electronic flight instrumentation system (EFIS), is virtually identical to that fitted to the 757/767 series. The 'bookcase' on the right of the picture is where the flight engineer's station was situated on earlier 747s

Above The Pratt & Whitney PW4056 turbofans which power this Singapore Airlines 747-400 'Mega Top' are each rated at 252.4 kN—equivalent to 56,000 lb of thrust at sea level. These fuel-efficient, high-bypass engines enable the aircraft to cruise comfortably at over eight miles a minute, nearly eight miles above the earth

Right the main gear doors are about to snap shut as Singapore Airlines 9V-SQS climbs out

Below The main panel of the Dash 400 is dominated by large CRT screens which display virtually all the data required by the crew as they operate the flight. An engine indication and crew alerting system (EICAS) is incorporated to issue caution and warning alerts to both the handling and non-handling pilot. EICAS also provides 'troubleshooting' information for maintenance personnel

Left and above Handsomely repainted from nose to tail, this 1974-vintage 747-100 is operated by Continental Airlines (now controlled by Scandinavian Airlines System)

Overleaf, left With the copilot at the helm, a Swissair 747-300 descends over the wide mouth of the River Plate as it approaches Buenos Aires, the capital of Argentina. The river's murky appearance is caused by its shallowness and fast currents—not pollution

Overleaf, right Long finals into Buenos Aires: the runway looks pitifully short from this distance (about two miles); as the airport is virtually at sea level, and the air temperature is around 20°C, this Dash 300 should be able to come to a stop after a 2000-m ground roll

SEAT MUST BE
IN FORWARD 7 INCHES OF TRAVEL
DURING TAKE-OFF AND LANDING

LIFE VEST

Above More dependable Pratt & Whitney power in the form of JT9D-7R4G2 turbofans attached to a Swissair 747-300. The broad sweep of the one-and-only Copacabana Beach is visible beyond the inboard engine as the Jumbo departs from Rio de Janeiro, Brazil en route for Buenos Aires

Right In common with most 747 operators, Swissair now cossets its first-class passengers in a partitioned compartment in the nose, the original bar and lounge in the upper deck being deleted in favour of additional economy-class seating

Left Turn-around time for a Varig 747-200B at the Brazilian flag carrier's Rio de Janeiro hub; PP-VNB is one of many 747s converted to Combi ('Combination') configuration, and features a strengthened main deck cargo floor, aft main deck cargo floor (port side) and specialized loading/unloading equipment

Above Another turn-around scene—this time involving a 747-300 of Holland's KLM. 'The Flying Dutchman' was an early customer for the Dash 300; production of this version has ceased in favour of the Dash 400. Boeing had delivered over 800 Jumbos by the beginning of 1991, of which 62 were Dash 300s and nearly 90 were Dash 400s

Left Next stop Schipol, Amsterdam as this KLM Dash 300 rotates. Even now, the sight of a 747 slipping the surly bonds is still a head-turner, if not a downright religious experience. On 9 February 1969, the prototype 747 needed only 1370 m of Paine Field's runway (adjacent to what was then the world's largest building in terms of volume—the 747 final assembly hall at Everett, Washington), to become airborne on her historic maiden flight

Above When an airline pilot qualifies for the flight deck of a 747, he or she will be at the top of their profession in more ways than one—no other jetliner will look down on the crew of this Korean Air Dash 300

Left Air France utilizes its fleet of early 747-100s on charters and inclusive tour flights. These holidaymakers are deplaning at the French Mulhouse half of the jointly operated Swiss/French Basel-Mulhouse Airport

Below Endangered species. The flight engineer (mostly out of shot), reads aloud the check list as a British Airways 747 lets down through the clag into London Heathrow. As it is impractical to retrofit the Dash 400's two-man cockpit into earlier models, flight engineers can look forward to a reasonably secure future as far as the 747 is concerned

Heathrow's Terminal 4, dominated by an impressive line up of British Airways 747s, TriStars and Concordes, is exclusive to the UK flag carrier; the 'foreign' Boeing 737 is not an interloper as KLM is one of a handful of other airlines which British Airways allows to use the terminal. 'T4' boasts the largest area of carpeting inside any single building in the world—and presumably also has an equally impressive army of vacuum cleaners!

Top left A 747-200B of South African Airways is towed to British Airways' Cranebank engineering facility at Heathrow; BA is entrusted with the maintenance of 747s and other jetliners operated by several foreign carriers

Bottom left After its Jumbos had sat on the ground for many months due to separate (though related) industrial disputes with its pilots and flight engineers, British Airways finally managed to introduce their 747s into service on 25 April 1970. This RB211-powered 747-200B is trundling along one of Heathrow's numerous taxiways

Above British Airways was the first 747 customer to specify Rolls-Royce RB211 turbofans, but this example is one of the carrier's original Pratt & Whitney JT9D-powered Dash 100 models. The forward-retracting nose gear is apparent as *City of Swansea* climbs away from Heathrow

A carrier which very much reflects the marketing talents of its dynamic proprietor, Richard Branson, Virgin Atlantic Airways has established an enviable reputation for affordable, high quality transatlantic services. *Maiden Voyager* (left), the first of Virgin's six pre-owned 747s, is being turned-around at London Gatwick before departing for New York (Newark)—where *Scarlet Lady* is preparing for a nighttime push back

Left You can almost hear the whine of those Pratt & Whitneys as this Jumbo
intimidates the photographer

Above Historically a loyal Douglas customer, Alitalia—in common with other
flag carriers—had no alternative but to sign with Boeing so as to stay
competitive on long haul routes. This General Electric CF6-powered Dash 200B
is in landing configuration with leading edge slats, double-slotted Fowler flaps
and gear deployed

Above and opposite On finals to London Gatwick after a flight from Bejing via Sharjah in the United Arab Emirates, B-2442 is a 747SP (Special Performance) model operated by the Civil Aviation Administration of China

Overleaf The days of *City of Gold Coast-Tweed*, a beautiful RB211-powered 747SP, were numbered as soon as Qantas took delivery of the even longer range Dash 400. As well as its shortened fuselage (ending with a distinctive 'kink'), the SP has a taller fin and an extended tailplane to counteract the aircraft's reduced moment arm

When it takes delivery of its first 747-400F freighter in late 1991, Cathay Pacific
will be operating five different 747 versions—all RB211-powered, naturally.
VR-HON, one of Cathay's original Dash 200Bs, shares the concrete at
Melbourne with a Qantas 747 and 767

Luxair's 747SP—operated by its subsidiary, Luxavia—is cossetted before
departing Luxembourg for Johannesburg, South Africa. Designed for long 'thin'
routes, the SP was launched in September 1973 and can carry 305 passengers
over 9660 km. Pan American successfully introduced the 747SP on its New
York – Tokyo route, but the market for this highly specialized jetliner proved
to be (at 45 aircraft), disappointingly small

A 747-300 from the land of the rising sun makes its final approach in the golden afterglow as the sun sets over London Heathrow. To describe Japan Air Lines as a major 747 customer is like saying that The Beatles were a successful pop group—at the beginning of 1991, JAL operated five 747-100; one 747-100B; one 747-100B (F); two 747-100B (SR); five 747-100B (SR/SUD); 23 747-200B; one 747-200B (F); eight 747-200F (SCD); nine 747-300; four 747-300 (SR/SUD); and ten 747-400 with no less than 30 more Dash 400s on order

Above Who needs passengers? United Parcel Service is one of the world's top ten cargo carriers; its fourteen 747s are fully occupied in handling the huge volumes involved in the small package industry. This 747-100F is caught on turn-around at Ontario Airport, California

Right *Prins van Oranje*, one of a pair of 747-200Cs operated by Martinair Holland, swallows part of a 125-tonne consignment at Amsterdam

Above Cargolux Airlines International was formed in 1970 and operates three 747-200Fs from Findel Airport, Luxembourg. Thanks to the freighter's upward-hingeing nose and specialized lifting equipment, cargo is easily loaded into the main deck. Interestingly, first class passengers are carried in the upper deck

Right No engine accessibility problems here as a Cargolux engineer inspects a General Electric CF6-50C2 turbofan 'on-wing'

No airline can afford to keep its aircraft sitting on the ground for long; after waiting for better visibility, this Dash 200F departs into milky skies. Cargolux has secured delivery positions for six 747-400Fs, the first of which is expected in 1994. Until then, the carrier's trusty Dash 200s will continue to serve Abu Dhabi, Dubai, Bangkok, Hong Kong, Singapore, Taipei and Fukuoka in the Far East, and Miami, Seattle and San Francisco across the North Atlantic. Cargolux raised a few eyebrows in 1990 when it concluded a charter agreement with Luton-based Air Foyle to hire an Antonov An-124 *Ruslan*—the largest aircraft in commercial service—in an attempt to capture a larger slice of the outsize cargo market on Asian routes

757 and 767: Boeing's Twin Peaks

British Airways was instrumental in launching the 757, signing firm contracts alongside Eastern Air Lines for a total of 88 aircraft (including 42 options), in May 1979. Uniquely Rolls-Royce achieved launch engine status on an all-new Boeing jetliner with the RB211-535C. BA's 39 Dash 200s are used intensively on European routes

Above When deliveries are complete, Air Europe will operate a fleet of 26 757-200s. To enhance the passenger appeal of this sleek jetliner, Boeing have redesigned the cabin to widen the aisle and improve the head and elbow room at window seats. After some notably lean years by Boeing standards, 757 sales recovered strongly in the airliner boom of the late eighties; by the start of 1991, over 300 757s had been delivered and production was running at seven aircraft per month

Right A dynamic UK charter operator, Air 2000 travels to destinations in Europe, East Africa and North America. G-OOOD, one of nine 757-200s delivered to the carrier by the end of 1990, prepares to swing across to its stand at Manchester International Airport

F-GCBD

Left TACA International Airlines SA is the national airline of El Salvador in Central America; pride of its compact Boeing fleet is this single 767-300ER. The carrier operates regular services between the capital, San Salvador, and Miami International Airport—where standard LD2 cargo containers are being unloaded from the 767's belly hold. TACA was one of the first airlines in Central America to receive jet equipment, having only recently disposed of its two original BAC One-Elevens

Below Luton-based Monarch Airlines operates an interesting mix of Airbus and Boeing equipment, including A300-600Rs and 757-200ERs; two 767-300ERs were ordered in 1990. G-MONK, a standard 757-200, was a distinctly unfamiliar sight in the deep blue skies of Australia when Monarch (and other UK carriers), helped to maintain air services during the industrial dispute between management and flight deck crews which grounded both Ansett and Australian Airlines for much of 1989/90

A LAN-Chile 767-299ER noses out of Miami before heading south for Santiago. The first 767-200 made its maiden flight in September 1981 and entered service with United Airlines in August 1982. Gross weights have climbed from 136,000 kg on the initial models to 156,500 kg for the Dash 200ER, which has a range of 14,250 km. A twin-aisle widebody, the 767 can accommodate up to 290 passengers in a variety of layouts: 747-type sleeper seats five abreast; medium-range six-abreast in first class; seven-abreast in economy class; and two-four-two eight-abreast in inclusive tour configuration

Below In common with the Airbus A310 and A300-600, ER versions of the 767 are capable of extended-range twinjet operations (ETOPS), over routes previously only flown by trijets or four-engined airliners. ETOPS modifications required by the Federal Aviation Administration (FAA), were increased fire suppression for the lower deck holds, additional equipment-overheat detectors and a fourth electric generator powered by a hydraulic motor. The 767-200ERs of Trans World Airlines (pictured), have been so modified by Boeing to allow flights over the North Atlantic and other oceans along tracks up to three hours single-engined flying time away from the nearest suitable diversion airfield

Right A US mega-carrier, United Airlines operates 20 767-200s and is taking delivery of sixteen 767-300ERs. United is one of Boeing's biggest customers with 370 aircraft already on firm order or optioned; by 1996, the airline expects to be operating 54 DC-10s and no less than 599 assorted Boeings. This standard 767-200 is about to make a copybook landing at New York's La Guardia Airport

Typical hustle on the ramp at Hong Kong's increasingly crowded Kai Tak; the scene is dominated by the uninspired livery of a Japan Air Lines 767-200, but an All Nippon Airways TriStar, Air India Airbus A300B4, Cathay Pacific TriStar and 747—even a Royal Hong Kong Auxiliary Air Force Beech Super King Air—are all in there somewhere

Guided by a Volkswagen 'Follow Me' van and escorted by two armoured vehicles, a 767-200ER of Israeli flag carrier El Al prepares to complete a scheduled flight from Tel Aviv. The outbreak of the Gulf War in January 1991 increased the threat of terrorist reprisals against American and British international carriers as well as El Al; combined with the general economic recession in the West, this caused a dramatic decrease in the number of airline passengers travelling between the US and Europe

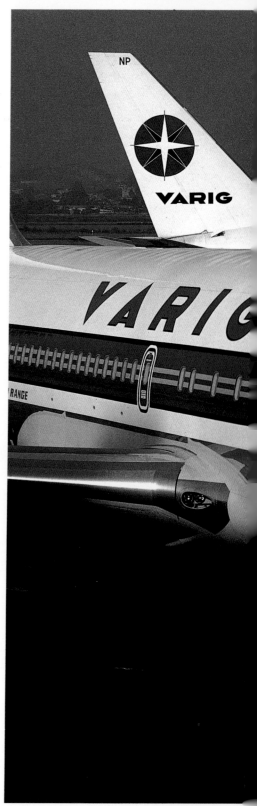

Above As the wet taxiway dries out, a Qantas 767-200ER faces brilliant sunshine and a beckoning sky

Right Brazil's Viação Aérea Rio-Grandense (Varig), was founded in 1927 with the technical assistance of the German Condor Syndicate. In addition to its ten 767-200ERs (two of which are seen here at Rio de Janeiro), the carrier has also signed for the Dash 300ER, which offers an increase in gross weight to 170,450 kg and a maximum range of 13,300 km. Thankfully, Varig has not succumbed to the 'white is right' doctrine of airline livery design which has afflicted other major international airlines

Most of the 330 767s delivered by early 1991 were extended range models; Boeing has proposed long range (LR) versions of the Dash 200/300 as a result of customer interest. Formed in 1940 as what would today be called a fixed base operator (FBO), Piedmont began scheduled local services in 1948. Administered from North Carolina, the carrier built up a solid route network and acquired the Utica, New York, based Empire Airlines in January 1986. Piedmont officially merged with USAir in August 1989 and lost its separate identity

DC-10 and TriStar:
The Big Trijets

Unlike the TriStar, the DC-10's centre engine is completely incorporated into the fin structure from where it enjoys uninterrupted air flow high above fuselage blanking effects. The rear view of this Lufthansa DC-10-30 (D-ADAO *Leverkusen*), reveals the geometry of the inboard trailing edge and the belly landing gear leg required by the heavier Dash 30 model, which has a maximum take-off weight (MTO), of 263,636 kg

Above British Airways became the operator of eight DC-10-30s when it absorbed British Caledonian. Gears travelling, G-NIUK *Cairn Edward Forest* departs London Gatwick for Los Angeles

Right The flight deck of the DC-10 is roomy and provides excellent visibility—especially from the large side windows. Most crews enjoy flying the big Douglas and praise its logical instrument layout and fine handling qualities. BA's G-BEBM is maintaining 260 knots indicated airspeed (KIAS), at flight level 350 over the heart of North America

Overleaf, left A close up of 'Bravo Mike's' main panel, characterized by the central group of performance indicators and the three power levers for its General Electric CF6-50C2 turbofans, each rated at 234 kN (52,500 lb)

Overleaf, right The DC-10 has a large and complex flight engineer's station; fuel used and fuel remaining (in pounds) is indicated on the panel above 'Bravo Mike's' operating manual

The DC-10 programme was launched in 1968 on the strength of large orders from American Airlines and United. Destined to be the last 'Douglas Commercial' family of airliners, which began with the DC-1 of 1933, the initial US domestic DC-10-10 model first flew in August 1970 and entered service with American one year later. The production list includes 120 DC-10-10s, nine DC-10-10CF, seven DC-10-15s, 174 DC-10-30s and Dash 30ERs, 23 DC-10-30CFs, twelve DC-10-30 Freighters, 41 DC-10-40s and 60 KC-10A Extender tanker/transports for the US Air Force. Production of civil models totalled 386; the last delivery (a Dash 30), was made to Nigeria Airways early in 1989. American Airlines maintains a fleet of 45 DC-10-10 'Luxury Liners'

Right The long-range DC-10-30 can carry a full payload over almost all airline sectors in the world. Bound for Miami, N68065 of Continental Airlines performs a brisk take-off from London Gatwick—sometimes referred to irreverently as 'Gatport Airwick!'

Below United Airlines operates 46 DC-10-10s on its extensive US domestic network. Although tempting, throttling back the trijets centre (No 2) engine in the cruise—whilst maintaining roughly normal power levels on the wing-mounted engines—does not improve fuel economy due to intake drag

Above Sundown at Dallas-Fort Worth, American Airlines' home and hub. The DC-10 was designed to combine coast-to-coast range for US domestic carriers with a passenger capacity of up to 380 in a high-density layout

Right Varig took delivery of the first of its ten DC-10-30s at the end of 1980; the Brazilian carrier also operates a pair of DC-10-30CFs

Left Parked at Heathrow, this DC-10-30 is the flagship of African carrier Ghana Airways; the rest of the fleet is comprised of single examples of the DC-9-50, Fokker F.28-2000 and F.28-4000

Above Helsinki-based Finnair operates a fleet of four DC-10-30s and a single DC-10-30ER; four MD-11s are on order. The fairing which extends above the jetpipe of the centre engine maximizes laminar flow at the rear of the nacelle, thereby reducing drag

Right Atlanta-based Delta Air Lines has 29 TriStars, including this L-1011 250—an upgraded TriStar 1. Designed in 1966–68 to meet the same requirement as the DC-10—the trunk route needs of US domestic carriers—the first L-1011 flew in November 1970, powered by Rolls-Royce RB211-22 turbofans. The subsequent development of the TriStar was critically delayed by the collapse of the original Rolls-Royce company in March 1971 (which had bled itself to death tackling the RB211's design problems), and Lockheed's own financial difficulties. Eventually, after delivering 249 TriStars, Lockheed decided to cut its losses and formally withdrew from airliner manufacture in 1981

Below A trio of trijets at Miami: an LTU Tristar 500 and an Eastern Air Lines TriStar 1/100 snuggle alongside a DC-10-30 of Venezuelan carrier Viasa

Eastern Air Lines was the first customer to sign for Lockheed's widebody and introduced the type into service on 15 April 1972. Arriving at New York La Guardia, N372EA was one of 24 TriStar 1s delivered to Eastern

Left Eastern joined the growing list of US airline casualties in January 1991, having failed to recover from a reported billion-dollar loss the previous year. The TriStars were put on the market before the carrier went under; N303EA was sold to International Air Leases in Florida

Above Five Star TriStar: the carrier's small L-1011 fleet is available for charters and operates on routes within the US, the Caribbean and Mexico

Above A British Airways TriStar joins a junior member of the fleet, a 757-200, and an Air UK Fokker F.27 Friendship at the holding point for runway 27R at Heathrow

Right Terminals 1 and 2, part of both main runways and the Cargo Centre (top of picture), are all visible in this view of Heathrow. The Air Canada TriStar 500 has just arrived from Toronto. In the 500 series, Lockheed certificated and delivered the first airliner featuring active controls. Optimized for long haul operations, the L-1011-500 was introduced in 1980 and has a shorter fuselage, extended wingtips and a computerized flight management system. By the time the RB211-524B4 was specified for the L-1011-500, Rolls-Royce's now supremely capable three-spool turbofan was being fitted to some 747s as well as every TriStar

Airbus: The European Giants

Left An Australian Airlines A300B4-203 makes an environmentally friendly approach into Melbourne Tullamarine

Below Star of Africa: one of Kenya Airways' three A310-300s slips into Heathrow after operating a flight from Nairobi

Right Pan American World Airways badly needed the operational efficiency of its large Airbus fleet to fight its financial crisis. This is *Clipper New York*, one of Pan Am's twelve A300B4-200s, rotating at La Guardia

Below After a ground roll of about 2850 m along Heathrow's runway 28L, the non-handling pilot will soon call 'V$_2$' (the take-off safety speed requried to overcome engine failure), as this Air France A300B2-101 establishes a positive rate of climb and accelerates to 165 kt. Since Air France inaugurated the first Airbus service on its Paris—London route in May 1974, the European consortium has delivered over 350 A300 twin-aisle widebodies

Above The long-haul A310 can accommodate 280 passengers and is available with a choice of General Electric CF6-50C2A2 or Pratt & Whitney PW4152 turbofans, rated at 237 kN (55,000 lb) and 231 kN (52,000 lb) respectively, offering a maximum payload range of 5450 km. In March 1990 the A300-600 and all A310 versions obtained EROPS certification from the Joint European Airworthiness Authorities and the FAA for flights over water up to 180 min from the nearest suitable diversionary airport. (A310s with PW4152 engines are cleared for 120 mins EROPS). KLM operates ten A310-200s

Right Two KLM A310-200s share their Schipol Amsterdam Airport base with a TWA TriStar and a Malaysia Airlines DC-10-30. Airbus predicts a market for over 6000 widebodies (some of which will replace DC-10s and Tristars), up to the year 2008, worth $450 billion at current prices

Right Emirates Airlines was created by the Dubai Government in 1985 and began operations using a 737-300 and an A300B4-200 wet-leased from Pakistan International Airlines. Despite the Gulf War, Emirates is determined to continue its fleet expansion programme; the carrier took delivery of the first of the three extended-range A300-600Rs in June 1990, and a further three extended-range A310-300s are expected to join A6-EKB in 1992–93

Below Air Seychelles leased this A300B4 to cater for increased holiday traffic

Above Eastern Air Lines' A300 order in July 1976 was a magnificent coup for Airbus Industrie. N233EA, along with fifteen A300B4-200s and five B4-100s, remained in the fleet until the carrier collapsed in January 1991. Note the line of Douglas DC-8s in the background as the aircraft departs Miami in happier times

Right French internal airline Air Inter operates six different Airbus models, including this cargo-swallowing A300B4-2C; fifteen A330s are on order. Interestingly, Air Inter continued to employ a dozen Caravelles at the end of 1990; the carrier also operates the entire production run of the Dassault Mercure short-range twinjet—eleven aircraft

Above Sporting Lufthansa's popular old colour scheme, this A300-600 taxies past a polizei MBB 105 helicopter at Stuttgart. The Dash 600 can accommodate 375 passengers and has a maximum payload range of 5350 km. Deutsche Aerospace is a partner in Airbus Industrie with Aérospatiale, British Aerospace and CASA, with Fokker and Belgian consortium Belairbus as an associate. At the end of 1990, Airbus had delivered over 650 aircraft with a further 1690 (of which 658 were A320s) on firm order. According to Chief Executive Jean Pierson, Airbus made a profit in 1990—twenty years since its formation—after breaking even in 1989

Opposite page Wardair A310-304s departing (top) and arriving at London Gatwick before the charter operator merged with Canadian Airlines International in 1990

Above Jordan's support for Iraq during the Gulf War had serious economic implications for the national carrier. Already shouldering a huge debt, Royal Jordanian was powerless to prevent major losses on its winter tourism and charter business. Hopefully, the A310-300s will be able to operate on high yield routes

Right With the exception of African routes, American Airlines operates worldwide. In addition to its 30-plus A300-605Rs, the carrier's widebodied fleet mix includes three versions of the 767 and DC-10

Above The beams from the nose gear landing lights of this A320 were so strong that the pilots of Norman Pealing's B-25 camera ship reported that their cockpit lighting had never been better!

Right An Airbus family gathering over the French Pyrenees: an American Airlines A300-605R leads a Royal Jordanian A310-300 and an Ansett Airlines of Australia A320-200

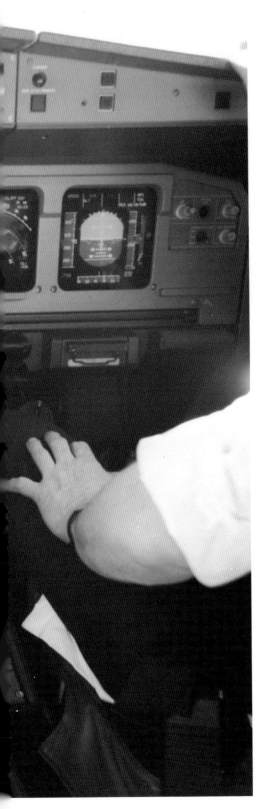

The world's first full-authority fly-by-wire airliner, the A320 flies with unbelievable precision. This masterpiece of high-technology features large colour electronic displays and sidestick controllers. Visibility through the deep windscreen is exceptional—a key attribute in today's crowded skies. Launched in 1984, the A320 has won more sales in the first six and half years of its existance than any other jetliner. Firm orders for the A320 and its stretched (180-seat) derivative, the A321, passed the 800 mark at the start of 1991

Soviet Superstars

The Antonov An-124 transport's awe-inspiring, semi-aerobatic display at the Australian Bicentennial Airshow in 1988 included wing-overs which progressed beyond the vertical. The MiG-29's Farnborough tailslide had nothing on this!

Above Designed to carry a 250,000 kg payload over 4500 km , the Antonov An-225 Mriya ('Dream') became the heaviest aircraft yet flown on 21 December 1988. Mriya has much in common with the An-124, including six of the same 230 kN (51,650 lb)-thrust Lotarev D-18T turbofans and an identical type of fly-by-wire control system. The An-225 made its Western debut at the Paris Salon in 1989, carrying the Soviet space shuttle orbiter Buran

Right and overleaf The flight deck of the An-225 is remarkably simple for such a gargantuan aircraft, and incorporates digital engine performance indicators in the centre of the main panel above the ground-mapping (left), and weather radar screens. Only a B-52 pilot has more power levers to operate. The two-seat flight engineer's station (**overleaf, right**), would not disgrace a nuclear power station!

The An-225's fuselage is based on that of the An-124 and has the same cross-section (6.4 m wide by 4.4 m high); the titanium cargo floor is 43 m long. The wing carries all six engines and spans 88.4 m

Above The tail section of the An-225, though similar to that of the An-124, is noticeably different, incorporating an increased-span tailplane with twin vertical fins at the tips

Right The fourteen, single-wheel main landing gears (each has an individual carbon-fibre door), are designed to cope with remote Siberian airfields, so arriving at Paris Le Bourget was a piece of cake. Antonov claims the An-225 can operate from a 1000-m runway, one third of the length required by the An-124. As well as carrying Buran ('Snowstorm'), the aircraft could also be used as the launch pad for BAe's HOTOL aerospacecraft

Left The Soviet Union's first widebody, the Ilyushin Il-86 first flew in December 1976, and scheduled services began in December 1980. The Il-86 has a gross weight similar to early-model DC-10s and TriStars (200,000 kg), but a limited production run of between 60 and 100 aircraft is indicative of its poor payload/range performance. CCCP-86088 replenishes at Heathrow

Below and overleaf The Il-96-300 can carry 300 passengers over 9000 km compared with Il-86's 3500 km range, due to its Soloviev PS90A turbofans and a lighter structure of new alloys and composites, combined with fly-by-wire and better aerodynamics, including winglets. The Il-96-300 made its maiden flight in October 1988

Last page Fin finale: the world's largest airline, Aeroflot also operates two of the world's largest aircraft—the Il-96-300 (foreground), and An-124